BRIAN AMBER.

EVIDENCE OF LOVE IN MARRIAGE

How to know if your husband or Wife truly love you.

Table of contents

Introduction

The Mandate of Mutual Love in Marriage

The order to a couple to show common love and steadfastness returns as of now to the hour of Paradise. In Genesis 2 the marriage association is portrayed as "becoming one tissue." And who, says Paul, has at any point couldn't stand his own tissue? You feed and support your own tissue. From the start it has been God's expectation that couple would cherish one another and be dedicated to each other (Eph. 5:28).

In a marriage there should be a functioning discussion. In any case, before they even start to see it, a couple will wind up turning out to be commonly alienated from each other. How might you keep on adoring your better half when you don't implore along with her? When you don't actually have any acquaintance with her? When you don't have the foggiest idea how she will respond to specific things? When you don't have the foggiest idea how you can satisfy her, or the things that bother her?

Luckily we get increasingly more writing that can be useful in these issues. Material, for instance, that focuses to the various manners by which married couples manage struggle, or how they experience their sexuality. What a ton of disappointments and strains can be caused through such contrasts! There are men who bypass their squabbles and don't manage the genuine issues. Or on the other hand ladies who on account of unsettled squabbles are not in that frame of mind to have sex. Much could be expounded on such matters, however we will allude them to books of individuals who are more learned around here. What concerns us currently is to show a couple of scriptural rules. Genuine love is coordinated to individuals of flesh. You love the other how the person is. You don't adore the "sovereign of your fantasies" yet the man you wedded. Love doesn't change the other as indicated by one's own preferences, however adjusts itself to the next with every one of their issues and inadequacies. "It isn't self-important or inconsiderate.

Chapter 1

What is a basic definition of love.

Love is an extreme, profound warmth for someone else. Love additionally means to feel this serious warmth for somebody. Love can likewise allude to serious areas of strength for a for something or to like something a great deal. Love has numerous different faculties both as an action word and a thing.

It is challenging to make sense of what love is. Love is quite possibly of the most serious feeling people feel throughout everyday life. It is something contrary to loathe, another unimaginably extraordinary inclination. At the point when you would do anything for a particular individual, that is normally on the grounds that you have affection toward them.

There are numerous sorts of profound warmth you can have for someone else, and they can be in every way depicted as affection. The adoration you feel for your folks won't be a similar love you feel for a dear companion or a significant other. You can likewise have serious areas of strength for a bond with a creature, like your canine. That, as well, is love. Mates ideally have affection for one another. It is normal that Husband and spouse should cherish each other even prior to getting married.True love, the sort of affection that holds a couple together for a lifetime, isn't an inclination yet a mentality. According to it, With the assistance of God, I will give my very best for upgrade the existence of my companion. Love is a natural feeling we feel in our Heart towards another person. We say it natural feelings because it not compulsory something has to be attached to it before you can say you love each other.

Chapter 2

How to truly love your spouse.

Genuine romance, the sort of adoration that holds a couple together for a lifetime, isn't an inclination yet a demeanor. According to it, "With the assistance of God, I will give my very best for upgrade the existence of my mate."

A man sat in my office and said, "I simply don't cherish my significant other any longer. I wish I did, however I don't. I've even requested that God give me love for her. However, I simply have no affections for her any longer."

This spouse was totally genuine, yet he was off track in how he might interpret love. He imagined love as warm, profound, heartfelt affections for his better half.

Since these didn't exist, he was unable to produce them and even God was not giving them, he presumed that his marriage was finished. Large number of people in our general public have reached a similar resolution.

Genuine romance, the sort of adoration that holds a couple together for a lifetime, isn't an inclination yet a demeanor. According to it, With the assistance of God, I will give my very best for upgrade the existence of my mate.

This disposition prompts words and activities that are useful to your companion and frequently animate warm feelings inside the life partner's heart. Assuming this individual responds with words and conduct that express their adoration for you, warm feelings may likewise get back to you.

One of the incredible misfortunes of Western culture

is that we have likened love with warm profound sentiments. Truth be told, these warm heartfelt sentiments are the consequence of adoration, not the quintessence of affection. To this end love can be directed, as in Ephesians 5:25: "Spouses, love your wives"; and adore can be educated and scholarly, as verified in Titus 2:4, where the more seasoned ladies are told to train the more youthful ladies to cherish their husbands. God doesn't order feelings, however He frequently orders perspectives and conduct.

Fortunately anything God orders, He empowers us to do.The connection among a couple is both intimate and procreative. Intimate common love and devotion is the unitive part of marriage. The procreative part of marriage concerns the origination, birth, and schooling of kids. The connection between the unitive and procreative may not be broken.

Trust is the bedrock of a marriage or any relationship besides. In the event that you're with a person who ends up adhering to his words, doesn't lie or conceal things from you, and makes you keep thinking about whether his affections for you tell the truth, he is a manager.

These can be indications of a decent man to wed. With a dependable person like him, you don't need to stress over his location when he is out on the grounds that you can trust him.

Trust is a two-way road, and a dependable person realizes that he can trust you too in Marriage.

Ask 1,000,000 individuals what makes a man a decent spouse material, and you'll find 1,000,000 distinct solutions.

However, there are a couple of characteristics and qualities that nearly everybody needs in their future spouses, making a person hubby material.

What are those characteristics, you could inquire? You take a gander at the person you're dating and ask yourself, 'would he say he is marriage material?'

or 'am I with some unacceptable individual?

By definition, is somebody you'd consider adequate to use the remainder of your coexistences. Be that as it may, what makes a man decent spouse material? Are the characteristics of a decent spouse learned or intrinsic?

Indeed, a few men treat their connections more in a serious way all along. They don't date to have some good times and bounce starting with one relationship then onto the next when things quit being entertaining. They put exertion into their relationship to overcome difficult stretches and need to get hitched.

Then again, a few people might like having somebody in their life however could do without getting hitched. They could favor a live-in relationship and can cheerfully live together with their accomplice however don't have any desire to get hitched not long from now or ever

While they sure have their reasons, and nothing bad can be said about not having any desire to get hitched, it could make you extremely upset if you have any desire to get hitched some time or another and as of now arranged a wedding in your mind.

Thus, right on time into the relationship, you ought to

watch out for signs in the event that the person is marriage material or not. A person who doesn't regard you or treat you well and possibly shows up when advantageous, regardless of how genuinely appealing he is, isn't hubby material.

Likewise, it relies upon what you're searching for in a person. Your dearest companion's meaning of amazing spouse probably won't match yours.

Be that as it may, assuming he is developed, stable, doesn't fear responsibility, and ready to remain on the special raised area or any place you choose to get hitched with you sooner or later, he merits an opportunity.

He acknowledges you as what your identity is

We as a whole have our deficiencies and characteristics. In the event that a person knows yours and acknowledges them without passing judgment on you, he is a trick.

You'll feel good in your skin when you're with him. Since he loves and regards you for who you genuinely are.

He moves you to be your best self

While he cherishes you for what your identity is and doesn't maintain that you should change, being with him makes you need to be a superior 'you' consistently.

He believes you should seek after your most out of this world fantasies, end your vices and keep up with the sound way of life you've for a long time truly cared about.

He pushes you to exceed everyone's expectations to your benefit. The manner in which he carries on with his own life and treats you makes you believe that should do likewise for him.

Wife's should also learn to love their husbands and treat them with a maximum respect.

Chapter 3

Qualities of Husband who love their Wife

1. Remembers his better half for imagining what's to come.

2. Will say "Please accept my apologies" and "Pardon me" to his loved ones.

3. Talks about family obligations with his significant other and ensures they are genuinely circulated.

4. Looks for meeting from his better half on all significant supporting choices.

5. Completely finishes responsibilities he has made to his significant other.

6. Expects the various stages his kids will go through.

7. Expects the various stages his marriage will go through.

8. Oftentimes lets his better half know what he prefers about her.

9. Gives monetarily to his family's fundamental everyday costs.

10. Manages interruption so he can converse with his better half and family.

11. Supplicates with his significant other consistently.

12. Starts significant family customs.

13. Starts fun family excursions consistently.

14. Sets aside some margin to give his youngsters viable guidance about existence.

15. Deals with the timetable of the home and expects pressure focuses.

16. Keeps his family monetarily sound and out of destructive obligation.

17. Ensures he and his better half have drawn up a will.

18. Gives his better half and youngsters access to the inside of his life.

19. Acknowledges profound obligation regarding his loved ones.

20. Respects his significant other in broad daylight.

21. Clarifies sex for every kid such that gives them a healthy viewpoint.

22. Urges his better half to develop as a person

23.Takes the lead in laying out sound family values.By botch, many couples don't kiss each other when they feel like they are excessively occupied, which can truly hurt their relationship. Try not to dismiss your significant other when he kisses you on the mouth. Those kisses are his desired image you, yet in addition that he cherishes you. Try not to allow those sentiments to blur.

24 He lets you know the amount he cherishes you.

He leaves the captions and the unobtrusive messages to the

side so he can straightforwardly let you know the amount he reveres you. He needs you similarly as on your big day.

25.He looks at you without flinching when you are together

At the point several's eyes meet during private minutes, it shows your longing for one another, yet in addition those profound sensations of affection. Assuming your significant other still looks at you without flinching, you can be sure that actually needs you and loves you with his entire existence.

26.He commendations your clothes

He makes a special effort to praise what varieties compliment you. He likewise could urge you to purchase new garments or notice how great you thoroughly searched in a dress you wore to the work party. These sort of remarks are inconspicuous signs that your significant other is still predominantly drawn to you.

Chapter 4

How to Rekindle the Lost Love between Husband and wife

Jesus is the main darling you want; no one but He can fill you and meet your feelings. We were made to be filled by His adoration and no other love not even our better half's will satisfy us like God's.

Search for Things that Made You Fall in Love in the First Place

As life occurs, we as a whole will quite often change. Your significant other or Wife could have changed a little yet the individual as yet unchanged individual. Rather than seeing just his issues, search for the positive side of him the things that pulled in you when you were recently married.Don't Take Your accomplice for Granted

Your significant other or your better half is a gift from God. Except if you open up the person in question, the best side of your accomplice will stay under cover. Also, how would you open up your accomplice? By valuing the person in question, obviously!

It required me a long investment to begin valuing my significant other, however it did some incredible things for our marriage. Find opportunity to see the value in every one of the little things your significant other or spouse does, in light of the fact that what you have now is to be valued.

Try not to Push Your Expectations onto your better half or spouse alone.

This is by a wide margin the greatest misstep I've made in my marriage. Your significant other is not the slightest bit awesome, nor are you. Attempt to acknowledge him as he is, instead of pushing him to be the man you maintain that he should be. Let him know that you love him for what his identity is! There might be the point at which your accomplice accomplished something that hurt you, and never apologized for it. Perhaps they even keep on getting it done, notwithstanding you telling them that it irritates you. This can make you foster a harshness towards them, Spouses likewise begin amplifying or focusing in on their accomplice's slip-ups, classifying their blemishes, and building a case to use sometime in the not too distant future," she adds. "It is too simple when you live around other people with somebody to dissect them and get irritated at a portion of their propensities, when all things considered, truly, your accomplice likely consistently had these characteristics, in any event, when you originally fell head over heels." Instead of being basic, take a stab at treating your join forces with generosity, it's the way to keeping your adoration alive. "Research has shown that making additional caring moves really causes you to feel more enamored. In any communication with your accomplice, whether it's private or viable, attempt to be thoughtful by they way you articulate your thoughts, "This mellow your accomplice, even in warmed minutes. Proceeding to be cherishing and liberal has a gigantic result as it not just keeps love alive, it encourages a more profound degree of closeness. As per Everyday

Health, projection is a mental safeguard system wherein individuals blame others for acting or feeling a specific way on the grounds that really, they, at the end of the day, feel as such. Projection can originate from troublesome youth encounters that convey into adulthood. "A typical explanation couples become so basic towards their accomplice is on the grounds that they will quite often extend negative characteristics of their folks or early guardians onto their accomplices, They likewise will more often than not expect their accomplice will act in the same ways that hurt them before and frequently read or misread their accomplice's words and actions.What characteristics about your life partner do you respect or feel entertained by? "Assuming you like that they're courageous, continue to share new exercises, If you partake in their fun loving nature in your correspondence, support bantering and the sharing of novel thoughts. Assuming you esteem that they're warm and friendly, try to associate with them every day, as opposed to becoming involved with other commonplace things." Your better half or spouse will see the value to your advantage in getting things done with them that you realize they appreciate, and it's probably they'll do a similar right back for you.

Marriage is tied in with giving, however ensure you set aside opportunity for yourself, as well. "To have a decent marriage, you should be a decent you, "Figure out how to focus on and put limits around exercises that keep you solid and entire exercises like rest, unwinding, wellness, and time with companions." as such, recollect that planning "personal" time into your day isn't egotistical, it's a need. It will reinforce your relationship since you'll have a saner rendition of "you" to bring to the "us" condition. Invest some energy taking a gander at your relationship and sort out what parts work and what parts don't. Pause for a minute to envision an ideal day in your ideal relationship. What might this resemble? How might you and your accomplice connect? Then, at that point, make an arrangement of how you could get from point A (your ongoing reality) to point B (that ideal day). Get it on paper in the event that you really want to, begin breaking the issues into reduced down pieces and handling them each in turn.

Cash is perhaps of the greatest stressor in a marriage. Many couples stress and squabble about it continually. Assuming you observe that you and your companion are beginning to badger each other over cash, now is the right time to address it. We are at fault for something financial experts call 'uninvolved independent direction, Using Economics to Master Love, Marriage, and Dirty Dishes. "Couples need to make a functioning arrangement about how they will deal with their money.

One more extraordinary method for infusing more love and regard into marriage is by figuring out how to endure, appreciate, and acknowledge contrasts. Companions will dissent, and they will have clashing perspectives.

Tolerating, enduring, and regarding your accomplice's contemplations and assessments will prompt acknowledgment, and acknowledgment advances love. Conflicts are a piece of any marriage, yet the way that you manage conflict is the critical distinction between a sound and undesirable marriage.

Your accomplice has the option to their own perspective and sentiments. An absence of agreement shouldn't prompt you disparaging or harming your mate.

Be humanely inquisitive when you meet your accomplice. Look them in their eyes, keep an open heart, and recollect the things you value about your accomplice. Recollect that both you and your accomplice are doing all that can be expected from there, the sky is the limit or less are battling very much like you.

It requires a ton of exertion and persistence to keep up with deference through the course of a relationship. Treating your life partner discourteously, rudely, and adversely incites similar conduct in them.

Acknowledge your various perspectives, appreciate their bits of feedbacks, hold a discourse open to pursue choices together, and compromise when required .

Regard and love in a marriage are in many cases lost when accomplices attempt to change their companion. Endeavoring to change somebody just aims you to fail to focus on the higher perspective. As opposed to making it a highlight call your companion out when you can't help contradicting their way of behaving or letting them know the proper behavior, do your part, and really try to establish a conscious and cherishing climate.

This approach is viable in light of the fact that you are showing others how its done. Regard is many times returned when it is given. Attempting to change your mate, then again, makes pressure. At long last, as a wedded couple, you enjoy a few jobs that were deliberately or unwittingly settled upon by both of you. It is basic to recall that regardless of which job your accomplice plays you generally regard their endeavors.

For those experiencing issues making a more deferential environment, think about treatment. Treatment assists couples with talking about troublesome issues, resolve them, and opposite insolent ways of behaving.

www.ingramcontent.com/pod-product-compliance
Lightning Source LLC
LaVergne TN
LVHW080556160826
845677LV00010B/1876

* 9 7 9 8 8 4 6 1 4 1 7 1 1 *